Building a Healthy Family

EVENT EXPERIENCE

PARTICIPANT GUIDE

From Dr. Gary Chapman, author of
#1 *New York Times* bestseller *The 5 Love Languages*®

MOODY PUBLISHERS
CHICAGO

Edited by Joyce Li
Interior design: Puckett Smartt
Cover design: Kaylee Lockenour Dunn
Cover photo of mother and son copyright © 2025 by BONNINSTUDIO/Stocksy/ Adobe Stock (159061448). Photo of parents and daughter copyright © 2025 by Serhii/Adobe Stock (499873796). Photo of father and son copyright © 2025 by Lightfield Studios/Adobe Stock (292849865). Photo of children running copyright © 2025 by maxximmm/Adobe Stock (631491245). All rights reserved.

ISBN: 978-0-8024-3784-6

Originally delivered by fleets of horse-drawn wagons, the affordable paperbacks from D. L. Moody's publishing house resourced the church and served everyday people. Now, after more than 125 years of publishing and ministry, Moody Publishers' mission remains the same—even if our delivery systems have changed a bit. For more information on other books (and resources) created from a biblical perspective, go to www.moodypublishers.com or write to:

Moody Publishers
820 N. LaSalle Boulevard
Chicago, IL 60610

1 3 5 7 9 10 8 6 4 2

Printed in the United States of America

CONTENTS

SESSION 1

Five Traits of a Healthy Family 5

SESSION 2

The 5 Love Languages® of Children and Teenagers 15

SESSION 3

Initiating Positive Change 23

SESSION 4

Anger: How to Tame a Powerful Emotion 31

SESSION 5

The 5 Apology Languages 41

SESSION 1

Five Traits of a Healthy Family

Five Traits of a Healthy Family

TRAIT #1: A healthy family adopts an attitude of service.

Wives ___________________

> *Wives, submit yourselves to your own husbands as you do to the Lord.* – **Ephesians 5:22 (NIV)**

Husbands ___________________, ___________________

> *Husbands, love your wives, just as Christ loved the church and gave himself up for her.* – **Ephesians 5:25 (NIV)**

Children ___________________ and ___________________

> *Children, obey your parents in the Lord, for this is right.*
> **– Ephesians 6:1 (NIV)**

Fathers ___________________

> *Fathers, do not exasperate your children; instead, bring them up in the training and instruction of the Lord.*
> **– Ephesians 6:4 (NIV)**

Service is a _____________ of _______________.

> *Submit to one another out of reverence for Christ.*
> **– Ephesians 5:21 (NIV)**

Two Games to Foster Service Within the Family

1. **"I really appreciate that!"**

   Once a week, take a few minutes to go around the table. Each person should mention one way in which they served another family member. Those who were served can then express appreciation.

   - "One way in which I served you is . . ."
   - Response: "I really appreciate that!"

   When we are intentional about both serving and appreciating one another, an attitude of service is cultivated within the family.

   You can also take this time to come up with new ideas for how to serve one another in the future!

2. **"Do you know what I would like?"**

   - "I'd like for you to . . ."
   - Response: "I'll try to remember that."

Service Beyond the Family

1. **Daily Sharing Time**

   At regular intervals (this can be daily or once a week), go around the table and have each person share one way that they served someone outside the family.

   - "One act of service I did today is ______________________."

2. **Plan a Family Service Project**

   What is something you can do all together as a family to serve others?

TRAIT #2: In a healthy family, there is intimacy between the husband and wife.

. . . a man leaves his father and mother and is joined to his wife, and the two are united into one. **– Ephesians 5:31 (NLT)**

1. **Intellectual Intimacy** means sharing ______________________, ______________________, ______________________.
2. **Emotional Intimacy** means sharing ____________________.
3. **Social Intimacy** means sharing ____________________.
4. **Spiritual Intimacy** means sharing our ____________________ with God.
5. **Physical Intimacy** means sharing our ____________________.

TRAIT #3: A healthy family has parents who teach and train.

Fathers, do not provoke your children to anger by the way you treat them. Rather, bring them up with the training and instruction that comes from the Lord. **– Ephesians 6:4 (NLT)**

Nurture – Training by ____________________.

Admonition – Teaching by ____________________.

These must always go together!

This is best done in the context of ____________________.

TRAIT #4: In a healthy family, husbands are loving leaders.

Words for Husbands

- H ______________ **– Ephesians 5:23**
- S ________________ **– Ephesians 5:23**
- L ________________; G ______________ **– Ephesians 5:25–28**
- F ___________ and C ___________ for Wife **– Ephesians 5:29**
- L ________________ Parents **– Ephesians 5:31**
- L ___________ and L ___________ Children **– Ephesians 6:4**

Characteristics of a Loving Husband

1. A loving husband views his wife as a ________________.
2. A loving husband will _________________ with his wife.
3. A loving husband will put his wife at the ___________ of his _________________ list.
4. A loving husband will love his wife _________________.
5. A loving husband is committed to __________________ and __________________ his wife's needs.
6. A loving husband will seek to model his _________________ and _________________ values.

TRAIT #5: A healthy family has children who obey and honor their parents.

Obedience is a healthy word!

1. Obedience implies respect for ____________________.
2. Obedience builds ____________________.
3. Obedience builds ____________________.

How to Teach Obedience

1. By our ________________.
2. By letting them ________________ consequences.
3. By ________________ obedience.

Obedience Leads to Honor

Honor is ________________ more than ________________!

To summarize, what are 5 traits of a healthy family?

1. An attitude of ________________
2. ________________ between husband and wife
3. Parents who ________________ and ________________
4. Husbands who are ________________ ________________
5. Children who ________________ and ________________ parents

LET'S REFLECT

Take a few minutes to reflect on the things we've considered throughout this session. What inspired or engaged you most personally? What are you most eager or challenged to implement in your own life?

BOOK RECOMMENDATIONS

All book recommendations can be found at 5LoveLanguages.com.

5 Traits of a Healthy Family
by Gary Chapman

The Marriage You've Always Wanted
by Gary Chapman

A Simple Guide to a Better Marriage
by Gary Chapman & John Hinkley

101 Conversation Starters for Families
by Gary Chapman & Ramon Presson

101 More Conversation Starters for Couples
by Gary Chapman & Ramon Presson

101 Conversation Starters for Couples
by Gary Chapman & Ramon Presson

The DIY Guide to Building a Family That Lasts: 12 Tools for Improving Your Home Life
by Gary Chapman & Shannon Warden

Screen Kids:

5 Relational Skills Every Child Needs in a Tech-Driven World

by Gary Chapman & Arlene Pellicane

Grandparenting Screen Kids:

How to Help, What to Say, and Where to Begin

by Gary Chapman & Arlene Pellicane

Building Love Together in Blended Families

by Gary Chapman & Ron L. Deal

Sharing Love Abundantly in Special Needs Families

by Gary Chapman & Jolene Philo

Anger:

Taming a Powerful Emotion

by Gary Chapman

The Gift of Sex:

A Guide to Sexual Fulfillment

by Joyce J. Penner & Clifford L. Penner

SESSION 2

The 5 Love Languages® of Children and Teenagers

The 5 Love Languages® of Children

#1: Physical Touch

One day some parents brought their children to Jesus so he could touch and bless them. But the disciples scolded the parents for bothering him. When Jesus saw what was happening, he was angry with his disciples. He said to them, "Let the children come to me. Don't stop them! For the Kingdom of God belongs to those who are like these children. I tell you the truth, anyone who doesn't receive the Kingdom of God like a child will never enter it." Then he took the children in his arms and placed his hands on their heads and blessed them. **– Mark 10:13–16 (NLT)**

#2: Words of Affirmation

The tongue can bring death or life; those who love to talk will reap the consequences. **– Proverbs 18:21 (NLT)**

- Words of ______________________________
- Words of ______________________________
- Words of ______________________________

#3: Quality Time

Then he appointed twelve of them and called them his apostles. They were to accompany him, and he would send them out to preach. **– Mark 3:14 (NLT)**

- Giving your child your ____________________________ ____________________________.

#4: Receiving ____________________

Since he did not spare even his own Son but gave him up for us all, won't he also give us everything else?
– Romans 8:32 (NLT)

#5: Acts of ________________________

Dear children, let's not merely say that we love each other; let us show the truth by our actions. **– 1 John 3:18 (NLT)**

How to Discover a Child's Primary Love Language

1. Observe how they express love to ______________.
2. Observe how they express love to __________________.
3. What do they ________________ most often?
4. What do they _________________ about?
5. Give choices between two options.
6. Experiment!

How Love Languages Affect Discipline

1. L_____________ Discipline
2. B_____________ Discipline
3. More _________________ Discipline

What About Teenagers?

1. Differences
   - Move toward ______________________
   - Development of ______________________ thinking
   - Search for ______________________
   - Fluctuating ______________________
   - Coping with ______________________ changes

2. Does Their Love Language Change?

   YES or NO

However, you must learn new ______________________.

3. The Ingredients of Love
   - ______________________
   - ______________________
   - ______________________

   The opposite of **connection** is ______________________.

   The opposite of **acceptance** is ______________________.

   The opposite of **nurture** is ______________________.

LET'S REFLECT

Take a few minutes to reflect on the things we've considered throughout this session. What inspired or engaged you most personally? What are you most eager or challenged to implement in your own life?

BOOK RECOMMENDATIONS

All book recommendations can be found at 5LoveLanguages.com.

The 5 Love Languages®
by Gary Chapman

The 5 Love Languages® For Men
by Gary Chapman

The 5 Love Languages® of Children
by Gary Chapman & Ross Campbell

The 5 Love Languages® of Teenagers
by Gary Chapman

A Teen's Guide to the 5 Love Languages®
by Gary Chapman & Paige Haley Drygas

The 5 Love Languages Singles® Edition
by Gary Chapman

The 5 Love Languages® Military Edition
by Gary Chapman & Jocelyn Green

God Speaks Your Love Language®
by Gary Chapman

Things I Wish I'd Known Before We Became Parents
by Gary Chapman & Shannon Warden

Things I Wish I'd Known Before My Child Became a Teenager
by Gary Chapman

Choose Greatness
by Gary Chapman & Clarence Shuler

SESSION 3

Initiating Positive Change

Can one partner improve a marriage?

______________________!

How Do I Begin?

A **common response** is to describe the problem in terms of my

______________'s ____________________.

A **biblical response** is to "r____________________ the

p________________."

> *Judge not, that you be not judged. For with what judgment you judge, you will be judged; and with the measure you use, it will be measured back to you. And why do you look at the speck in your brother's eye, but do not consider the plank in your own eye? Or how can you say to your brother, "Let me remove the speck from your eye," and look, a plank is in your own eye? Hypocrite! First remove the plank from your own eye, and then you will see clearly to remove the speck from your brother's eye.* **– Matthew 7:1–5 (NKJV)**

Practice

1. Prayer: "Lord, what is wrong with __________?"

> *Search me, O God, and know my heart; try me, and know my anxieties; and see if there is any wicked way in me, and lead me in the way everlasting.*
>
> **– Psalm 139:23–24 (NKJV)**

Let all bitterness, wrath, anger, clamor, and evil speaking be put away from you, with all malice. And be kind to one another, tenderhearted, forgiving one another, even as God in Christ forgave you. **– Ephesians 4:31–32 (NKJV)**

2. Confession = "to ________________ with"

Agree with God that:

- It is ____________________
- Christ paid the ____________________
- We will accept His ______________________

If we confess our sins, He is faithful and just to forgive us our sins and to cleanse us from all unrighteousness. **– 1 John 1:9 (NKJV)**

3. Restitution

Clear the ____________________.

I myself always strive to have a conscience without offense toward God and men. **– Acts 24:16 (NKJV)**

How Do I Continue in Growth?

A **common response** is: "TRY ___________________!"

A **biblical response** would be . . .

And do not be drunk with wine, in which is dissipation; but be filled with the Spirit. **– Ephesians 5:18 (NKJV)**

But the fruit of the Spirit is love, joy, peace, longsuffering, kindness, goodness, faithfulness, gentleness, self-control.
– Galatians 5:22–23 (NKJV)

A Principle to Remember

Be ____________________ (________________________) with the

________________ _________________.

His Light Shining Through Us

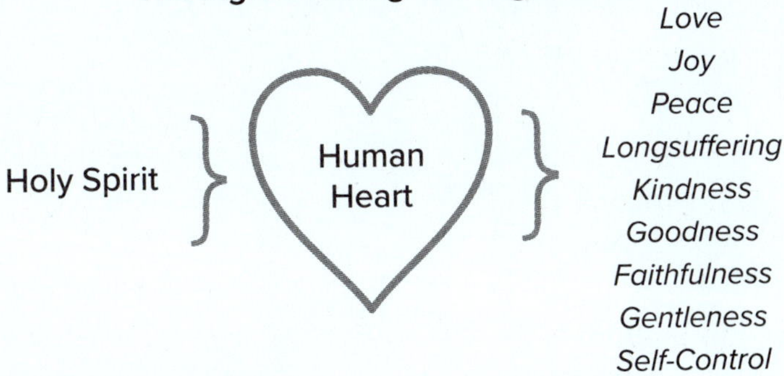

Ministry of the Holy Spirit

The Holy Spirit ____________________________ all Christians.

But you are not in the flesh but in the Spirit, if indeed the Spirit of God dwells in you. Now if anyone does not have the Spirit of Christ, he is not His.
– Romans 8:9 (NKJV)

The Holy Spirit ______________________ us when we do wrong.

And you have forgotten the exhortation which speaks to you as to sons: "My son, do not despise the chastening of the LORD, nor be discouraged when you are rebuked by Him."
– Hebrews 12:5 (NKJV)

The Holy Spirit ________________________ us of the truth.

However, when He, the Spirit of truth, has come, He will guide you into all truth; for He will not speak on His own authority, but whatever He hears He will speak; and He will tell you things to come. **– John 16:13 (NKJV)**

The Holy Spirit ________________________ us.

And I will pray the Father, and He will give you another Helper, that He may abide with you forever.
– John 14:16 (NKJV)

The Holy Spirit ________________________ the qualities of Christ through us.

But the fruit of the Spirit is love, joy, peace, longsuffering, kindness, goodness, faithfulness, gentleness, self-control. Against such there is no law.
– Galatians 5:22–23 (NKJV)

Two Essentials

1. ____________________ the Holy Spirit.
2. ____________________ to His control.

The Throne of the Heart

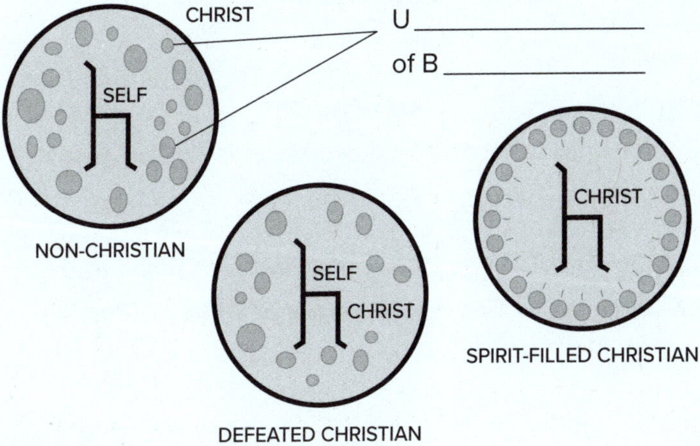

Let's Reflect

Take a few minutes to reflect on the things we've considered throughout this session. What inspired or engaged you most personally? What are you most eager or challenged to implement in your own life?

BOOK RECOMMENDATIONS

All book recommendations can be found at 5LoveLanguages.com.

Seen. Known. Loved.
5 Truths About God & Your Love Language®
by Gary Chapman & R. York Moore

5 Simple Ways to Strengthen Your Marriage . . .
When You're Stuck at Home Together
by Gary Chapman

Married and Still Loving It:
The Joys and Challenge of the Second Half
by Gary Chapman & Harold Myra

One More Try:
What to Do When Your Marriage Is Falling Apart
by Gary Chapman

Loving Your Spouse When You Feel Like Walking Away:
Real Help For Desperate Hearts in Difficult Marriages
by Gary Chapman

Holding on to Love After You've Lost a Baby
by Gary Chapman & Candy McVicar

The Love Language® Devotional Bible
by Gary Chapman

Your New Life with Adult Children:
A Practical Guide to What Helps,
What Hurts, and What Heals
by Gary Chapman

SESSION 4

Anger: How to Tame a Powerful Emotion

The Source of Anger

Anger is rooted in the nature of God.

God is ______________________________.

Whoever does not love does not know God, because God is love. **– 1 John 4:8 (NIV)**

God is _________________________________.

For it is written: "Be holy, because I am holy." **– 1 Peter 1:16 (NIV)**

Therefore, God is ____________________ with the wicked every day.

God is an honest judge. He is angry with the wicked every day. **– Psalm 7:11 (NLT)**

Why do we experience anger?

We are made in the __________________ of God.

So God created mankind in his own image, in the image of God he created them; male and female he created them. **– Genesis 1:27 (NIV)**

Therefore, we have a concern for ____________________ or ______________________.

We get angry when our sense of _________________________ is violated.

The Purpose of Anger

1. To motivate us to take ____________________ action.
2. God is our ____________________

   God punishes the ____________________

Dear friends, never take revenge. Leave that to the righteous anger of God. For the Scriptures say, "I will take revenge; I will pay them back," says the LORD. **– Romans 12:19 (NLT)**

The Lord isn't really being slow about his promise, as some people think. No, he is being patient for your sake. He does not want anyone to be destroyed, but wants everyone to repent. **– 2 Peter 3:9 (NLT)**

   Jesus corrected the ____________________

It was nearly time for the Jewish Passover celebration, so Jesus went to Jerusalem. In the Temple area he saw merchants selling cattle, sheep, and doves for sacrifices; he also saw dealers at tables exchanging foreign money. Jesus made a whip from some ropes and chased them all out of the Temple. He drove out the sheep and cattle, scattered the money changers' coins over the floor, and turned over their tables. Then, going over to the people who sold doves, he told them, "Get these things out of here. Stop turning my Father's house into a marketplace!" Then his disciples remembered this prophecy from the Scriptures: "Passion for God's house will consume me." **– John 2:13–17 (NLT)**

God announces impending ________________________

and provokes ________________________.

Therefore, go and give this message to Israel. This is what the LORD *says: "O Israel, my faithless people, come home to me again, for I am merciful. I will not be angry with you forever. Only acknowledge your guilt. Admit that you rebelled against the* LORD *your God and committed adultery against him by worshiping idols under every green tree. Confess that you refused to listen to my voice. I, the* LORD*, have spoken!"* **– Jeremiah 3:12–13 (NLT)**

"Who can tell? Perhaps even yet God will change his mind and hold back his fierce anger from destroying us." When God saw what they had done and how they had put a stop to their evil ways, he changed his mind and did not carry out the destruction he had threatened. **– Jonah 3:9–10 (NLT)**

3. Two types of human anger

- ________________________ **anger – a wrong has been committed**

But when Peter came to Antioch, I had to oppose him to his face, for what he did was very wrong. When he first arrived, he ate with the Gentile believers, who were not circumcised. But afterward, when some friends of James came, Peter wouldn't eat with the Gentiles anymore. He was afraid of criticism from these people who insisted on the necessity of circumcision. As a result, other Jewish believers followed Peter's hypocrisy, and even Barnabas was led astray by their hypocrisy. When I saw that they were not following the truth of the gospel message, I said to Peter in front of all the others, "Since you, a Jew by birth, have discarded the Jewish laws and are living like a Gentile, why are you now trying to make these Gentiles follow the Jewish traditions?" **– Galatians 2:11–14 (NLT)**

- **________________________________ anger – no wrong has been committed**

Abel also brought a gift—the best portions of the firstborn lambs from his flock. The LORD accepted Abel and his gift, but He did not accept Cain and his gift. This made Cain very angry, and he looked dejected. "Why are you so angry?" the LORD asked Cain. "Why do you look so dejected? You will be accepted if you do what is right. But if you refuse to do what is right, then watch out! Sin is crouching at the door, eager to control you. But you must subdue it and be its master." **– Genesis 4:4–7 (NLT)**

So Naaman went with his horses and chariots and waited at the door of Elisha's house. But Elisha sent a messenger out to him with this message: "Go and wash yourself seven times in the Jordan River. Then your skin will be restored, and you will be healed of your leprosy." But Naaman became angry and stalked away. "I thought he would certainly come out to meet me!" he said. "I expected him to wave his hand over the leprosy and call on the name of the LORD his God and heal me! Aren't the rivers of Damascus, the Abana and the Pharpar, better than any of the rivers of Israel? Why shouldn't I wash in them and be healed?" So Naaman turned and went away in a rage. **– 2 Kings 5:9–12 (NLT)**

This change of plans greatly upset Jonah, and he became very angry. . . . The LORD replied, "Is it right for you to be angry about this?" **– Jonah 4:1, 4 (NLT)**

The Process of Anger

1. ________________________ your anger

And "don't sin by letting anger control you." Don't let the sun go down while you are still angry . . . **– Ephesians 4:26 (NLT)**

Restrain your immediate ________________________

Sensible people control their temper. **– Proverbs 19:11 (NLT)**

2. Locate the ________________________ of your anger.

- Why am I angry?
- What wrong was committed?

3. If it is distorted anger: confess it as ____________________.

   Seek to negotiate ______________________.

   Accept their ______________________.

Always be humble and gentle. Be patient with each other, making allowance for each other's faults because of your love. **– Ephesians 4:2 (NLT)**

4. If it is definitive anger, take ____________________ action.

   Lovingly ______________________ the offender.

"If another believer sins, rebuke that person; then if there is repentance, forgive. Even if that person wrongs you seven times a day and each time turns again and asks forgiveness, you must forgive." **– Luke 17:3–4 (NLT)**

Dear brothers and sisters, if another believer is overcome by some sin, you who are godly should gently and humbly help that person back onto the right path. And be careful not to fall into the same temptation yourself. **– Galatians 6:1 (NLT)**

____________________ the person and your anger to God.

Dear friends, never take revenge. Leave that to the righteous anger of God. For the Scriptures say, "I will take revenge; I will pay them back," says the LORD. **– Romans 12:19 (NLT)**

He did not retaliate when he was insulted, nor threaten revenge when he suffered. He left his case in the hands of God, who always judges fairly. **– 1 Peter 2:23 (NLT)**

Alexander the coppersmith did me much harm, but the Lord will judge him for what he has done. Be careful of him, for he fought against everything we said. **– 2 Timothy 4:14–15 (NLT)**

Return ________________ for evil.

Instead, "If your enemies are hungry, feed them. If they are thirsty, give them something to drink. In doing this, you will heap burning coals of shame on their heads." Don't let evil conquer you, but conquer evil by doing good.
– Romans 12:20–21 (NLT)

Challenge

Learn to use the emotion of anger to ________________ the ________________ of Christ in the world.

Let's Reflect

Take a few minutes to reflect on the things we've considered throughout this session. What inspired or engaged you most personally? What are you most eager or challenged to implement in your own life?

BOOK RECOMMENDATIONS

All book recommendations can be found at 5LoveLanguages.com.

Anger: Taming a Powerful Emotion
by Gary Chapman

The 5 Apology Languages
by Gary Chapman and Jennifer Thomas

One More Try: What to Do When Your Marriage Is Falling Apart
by Gary Chapman

Loving Your Spouse When You Feel Like Walking Away: Real Help for Desperate Hearts in Difficult Marriages
by Gary Chapman

SESSION 5

The 5 Apology Languages

Two Essentials for Successful Relationships

1. That the individuals feel __________ and __________________.

2. That the individuals ___________ effectively with their __________________.

Whoever conceals their sins does not prosper, but the one who confesses and renounces them finds mercy.
– Proverbs 28:13 (NIV)

But your iniquities have separated you from your God; your sins have hidden his face from you, so that he will not hear.
– Isaiah 59:2 (NIV)

Therefore, if you are offering your gift at the altar and there remember that your brother or sister has something against you, leave your gift there in front of the altar. First go and be reconciled to them; then come and offer your gift.
– Matthew 5:23–24 (NIV)

Learning to Apologize

1. Where do we learn to apologize?

   Typically, from our ________________________.

2. What does a sincere apology look like?
   - When you apologize, what do you typically say or do?
   - When someone is apologizing to you, what do you want to hear them say or do?

What Are the 5 Apology Languages?

Expressing Regret

"I'm sorry that I ______________________________."

> *"I am no longer worthy to be called your son."* **– Luke 15:21 (NIV)**

> *A broken and contrite heart you, God, will not despise.*
> **– Psalm 51:17 (NIV)**

Accepting Responsibility

"I was wrong . . ."

> *"I have sinned against heaven and against you."* **– Luke 15:21 (NIV)**

> *If we confess our sins, [God] is faithful and just and will forgive us our sins.* **– 1 John 1:9 (NIV)**

Making Restitution

"What can I do to make this right?"

> *"Lord . . . if I have cheated anybody out of anything, I will pay back four times the amount."* **– Luke 19:8 (NIV)**

Genuinely Repenting

"I don't want this to keep happening."

> *"Repent and be baptized, every one of you, in the name of Jesus Christ for the forgiveness of your sins."* **– Acts 2:38 (NIV)**

Requesting Forgiveness

"Will you forgive me?"

> *. . . blot out my transgressions. Wash away all my iniquity and cleanse me from my sin.* **– Psalm 51:1–2 (NIV)**

Each of us has a primary apology language. If you want to communicate your sincerity, you must speak the other person's language.

Discovering Your Primary Apology Language

When I apologize, what do I typically say or do?

What hurts me most deeply about this situation?

What could they say or do that would make it easier for me to forgive?

Learning to Forgive

God is our ________________.

> *Be kind and compassionate to one another, forgiving each other, just as in Christ God forgave you.* **– Ephesians 4:32 (NIV)**

How does God forgive us?

> *If we confess our sins, [God] is faithful and just to forgive our sins.* **– 1 John 1:9 (NIV)**

What is forgiveness?

1. It is "to ____________________" or "to ________________ away"

> *". . . I will forgive their wickedness, and I will never again remember their sins."* **– Jeremiah 31:34 (NLT)**

He has removed our sins as far from us as the east is from the west. – **Psalm 103:12 (NLT)**

2. Forgiveness is a ________________ response to an apology.

What forgiveness does not do:

1. Forgiveness does not ________________ our memory.
2. Forgiveness does not remove all painful ________________.
3. Forgiveness does not remove all the ________________ of sin.
4. Forgiveness does not ________________ trust.
5. Forgiveness does not always result in ________________.

What if the person does not speak your apology language?

1. By nature, you will question their ________________.
2. By faith, you choose to ________________ them.

What if the person does not apologize?

1. We lovingly ________________.

"If another believer sins against you go privately and point out the offense. If the other person listens and confesses it, you have won that person back. But if you are unsuccessful, take one or two others with you and go back again, so that everything you say may be confirmed by two or three witnesses. If the person still refuses to listen, take your case to the church. Then if he or she won't accept the church's decision, treat that person as a pagan or a corrupt tax collector." – **Matthew 18:15–17 (NLT)**

2. We release that person to ________________.

He did not retaliate when he was insulted, nor threaten revenge when he suffered. He left his case in the hands of God, who always judges fairly. **– 1 Peter 2:23 (NLT)**

3. We ____________________ for them and stand ready to ________________.

4. We return ________________________ for evil.

Do not take revenge, my dear friends, but leave room for God's wrath, for it is written: "It is mine to avenge; I will repay," says the Lord. On the contrary: "If your enemy is hungry, feed him; if he is thirsty, give him something to drink. In doing this, you will heap burning coals on his head." Do not be overcome by evil, but overcome evil with good.
– Romans 12:19–21 (NIV)

Making It Personal

1. Whom do I need to forgive?
2. Whom do I need to lovingly confront?
3. Whom do I need to release to God?
4. To whom do I need to apologize?

Let's Reflect

Take a few minutes to reflect on the things we've considered throughout this session. What inspired or engaged you most personally? What are you most eager or challenged to implement in your own life?